CW00850585

strategies for
success

the evolving world of e-business –
how IT really can underpin your
business performance

consultant editor:	Marc Beishon
sub-editor:	Lesley Malachowski
production manager:	Lisa Robertson
design:	Halo Design
commercial director, DP Ltd:	Ed Hicks
commercial director, IoD:	Sarah Ready
publishing director:	Tom Nash
chief operating officer:	Andrew Main Wilson

Published for the Institute of Directors and Oracle
Corporation UK Ltd by Director Publications Ltd,
116 Pall Mall London SW1Y 5ED
T 020 7766 8950 W www.iod.com

Oracle's business is information – how to manage it, use it, share it, protect it. For nearly 30 years, Oracle, the world's largest enterprise software company, has provided the software and services that let companies get the most up-to-date and accurate information from their business systems. We offer a range of database, software development tools and business application software products, along with related consulting, education, and support services and have customers among the world's largest and most successful firms, through to over 80,000 SMEs.

As a growing business your primary concern is to grow profits by increasing operational efficiency and making better business decisions. To achieve this you may need to invest in IT as a strategic tool. Today, Oracle is helping both governments and businesses around the world to become information-driven by following three principles: simplify, standardise and automate.

Oracle's E-Business Suite provides a set of business applications that work with a single global database. It allows users to integrate and automate the flow of business processes across front and back-office functions, giving organisations a foundation for consolidated information such as sales positions, inventory levels and revenue across all lines of business, products and geographies.

E-Business Suite Special Edition is designed to make the software's capabilities available and affordable to SMEs. It is supplied pre-installed and pre-configured (using industry best practice business flows) in a commercial offering that includes hardware, software licences, implementation services, training and support. This means organisations can be up and running with an integrated set of financial, manufacturing, CRM, purchasing, order management, and inventory applications, and look to a fast return on investment, whilst reducing the risks inherent in traditional software implementations.

In addition, we offer organisations access to literally hundreds of partner solutions. This comprehensive portfolio of products, which spans across business functions and industry sectors, runs on the Oracle Database. This scaleable platform allows you to access insightful, real time data, which lets you see, understand and make informed decisions on your operation – when you want and how you want.

To see what impact today's IT can make to your business, take the Oracle healthcheck. Visit www.oracle.com/start and enter keyword 'success' or call 0870 876 8773.

CONTENTS

 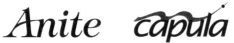 

delivering tangible benefits

**Miles Templeman, Director General
Institute of Directors**

Robert Solow, the nobel prize winning US economist, once famously observed that: "you can see the computer age everywhere but in the productivity statistics". This 'productivity paradox' was ultimately resolved through better research and measurement, demonstrating that (just occasionally) even the most eminent economist can be just plain wrong. Targeted investment in information and communications technologies (ICT) – allied with the careful redesign of business processes and investment in training and motivating staff in these new ways of doing business – can greatly enhance business performance. This feeds through directly into bottom-line benefits.

On the grand scale, investment in ICT is having a transformational impact on both productivity and growth. In the USA, such ICT investment produced an estimated one-percentage point increase in yearly GDP growth in each of the last ten years. There is every reason to expect this to continue for many years. Research suggests that Europe has been slower to extract these benefits, once again causing the productivity gap between us and the USA to widen.

At a more local level, IoD members are increasingly realising these benefits, with affordable broadband access seen as a key catalyst. In research carried out by the IoD and Nildram, published in October 2004, members emphasised the benefits being delivered by information systems enabled by broadband communications. More than 80 per cent of respondents indicated that they had seen quantifiable productivity benefits from such systems. Similarly, 33 per cent cited quantified improvement in customer satisfaction.

IoD research with Dell suggests that 73 per cent of small and medium enterprises (SMEs) also see productivity improvement as the key driver behind IT investment. They cited increasing sales, reducing cost, reducing risk and constructive response to competitive pressure as key benefits. And, 84 per cent saw ICT investment as vital to the growth plans for their businesses.

The vast majority of ICT investments are made to support business change programmes. All too many such investments in the past have failed to deliver the full benefits promised. Typically, this has been caused by an inability to focus on driving through the radical changes to business processes sought, and/or a failure to change pay and performance measurement systems to encourage the required new staff behaviours. These are failures of management rather than technology. In contrast, this guide provides clear and concise help on the steps required for success, particularly focusing on SMEs. I commend it to you.

helping SMEs
to play their part

Ian Smith, Senior Vice President and Managing Director, Oracle Corporation, UK, Ireland and South Africa

The size of the challenge facing UK SMEs today, which are competing in a global economy against low-cost rivals, should not be underestimated. They have to find new innovative ways to offer value and differentiation to their customers.

Technology has a key role to play in meeting this challenge, having already been proven to enhance the productivity and efficiency of companies across the world. IT can help these companies overcome major obstacles, such as constrained growth and pressure to maintain their position in the value chain. Technology can also be used to address several critical and complex issues, including financial regulatory compliance, recruitment and staff training procedures and managing supplier and customer relationships. However, let us not forget that UK SMEs do not have the luxury of endless resources to manage and exploit technology like their larger competitors. How do they identify IT solutions, which will help them to innovate the way they do business and stay ahead of the competition?

Oracle recognises that SMEs are integral to the UK economy. By supporting their efforts to innovate through IT we can help them to turn ideas into growth opportunities. There are already encouraging signs, with increasing numbers of UK companies adopting IT strategies to gain competitive advantage. But there are still barriers to overcome. In a DTI study on international benchmarking (2004), 77 per cent of UK firms were identified as having a business plan, but only 32 per cent had an IT policy as part of the overall strategy. This guide offers SMEs clear advice on how to adopt technology as part of their overall business strategy and to help ensure that small businesses remain a strong contributor to the UK's GDP.

Are you qualified to be a director?

EXECUTIVE DIRECTOR

FTSE 100 company wishes to appoint a Marketing Director to the board. The candidate must either be cogniscent with all aspects of company direction and hold the IoD Diploma in Company Direction or undertake the programme on appointment. All current members of the board are Chartered Directors and it is expected that the successful candidate will progress to C Dir status.

FINANCE DIRECTOR

Medium sized organisation seeks a qualified accountant who as a member of the board is also able to make a significant contribution to the overall development of the business. Accordingly, a Chartered Director is preferred, identifying a demonstrable track record of success in delivering profitable growth.

CHAIRMAN

International company requires a Chairman to lead investor relations and present to key financial institutions. The successful candidate will hold the IoD Diploma in Company Direction and be a Chartered Director, due to the high regard for these qualifications in the investment community.

NON-EXECUTIVE DIRECTOR

A major PLC is looking to expand its board with an experienced NED. The candidate must be a Chartered Director and therefore demonstrate the highest levels of strategic direction and the profile to communicate with shareholders.

CHIEF EXECUTIVE

This not for profit organisation is seeking an experienced chief executive possessing high standards of leadership and ability to guide the organisation through a period of restructuring and regional expansion. In addition, knowledge of and adherence to, sound corporate governance is essential. Only Chartered Directors will be considered for this position.

COMPANY SECRETARY

A FTSE 50 organisation seeks a company secretary who can demonstrate the experience and confidence to work with a high profile main board consisting of Chartered Directors. The successful candidate is also expected to contribute to the strategic direction of the company and be a senior team leader. Preference will be given to a Chartered Secretary who has also qualified as a Chartered Director.

These positions are fictitious but are representative of Chartered Directors and their organisations.

Chartered Director is the IoD's professional qualification for directors and receives the endorsement and support of government, regulators, the investment community, executive search agencies, the public sector and organisations including FTSE 100 companies.

To read some of the most recent Chartered Director success stories, visit www.iod.com/chartered

business and IT – setting the scene

While companies understand that IT can bring immediate bottom-line benefits, many are still failing to link their overall strategy to technology, says Marc Beishon, business and technology writer

One major software vendor, looking back over the effectiveness of its products, made the candid admission that – contrary to opinion – the vast majority of its installations were up and running – it was just that many were not being used for the purpose for which they were originally purchased. Much of those implementations were done in the scramble to put in new customer-facing systems in the late nineties, but times have changed.

Today, companies are looking for demonstrable value and return on investment for their IT purchases from the outset. They have recognised that technology is not a fashion accessory but an enabler of both immediate bottom-line benefits and new ways of working that, in time, could also lead to returns.

Nowadays there is much more awareness among companies about how IT fits into business, particularly when it comes to implementing certain types of system. Unfortunately, however, there is much less evidence of companies making a concerted attempt to link their overall business strategy to technology.

EXECUTIVE SUMMARY

- [ ] IT and business alignment is a highly complex issue
- [ ] increasingly more companies are using core financial metrics to measure the benefits of effective IT
- [ ] when IT and business goals are not aligned IT projects are more likely to fail
- [ ] finally, technology and business units are learning to work together

The latest DTI *International Benchmarking Study* (for 2004) – which covers information and communication technologies – provides important evidence of encouraging trends for UK businesses. The survey confirms that there has been a significant increase in the proportion of businesses that are measuring the benefits of IT using core financial metrics, such as return on investment, internal rate of return and net present value. It also reports that UK businesses are among the most likely to have written business plans and documented IT strategies. (However, this is not necessarily a good indicator as the number of those that have both is still relatively low. See chapter 2.)

IT adoption patterns

The most commonly cited reasons for UK businesses to adopt IT are to increase the efficiency of their processes, improve communication with customers, and to 'keep up with progress'. In particular, businesses are using technology to foster greater interaction with others as follows:

☐ more functionality and information are available online to customers

☐ more businesses are searching for and buying from suppliers online

☐ the proportional value of online sales and purchases has increased significantly

So, not surprisingly, much of the 'hard' indicator data about IT adoption involves communication technologies and online working. The DTI survey reports that:

☐ broadband adoption is accelerating – more than 60 per cent of UK businesses have Internet connections with a bandwidth of over one megabit/s

☐ UK businesses lead in wireless adoption – 28 per cent of businesses are using wireless networks in their premises, for example

☐ UK businesses are early adopters of new technologies, such as Internet telephony and desktop videoconferencing

There is also good news for smaller firms, which are catching up with larger companies in the implementation of websites and online trading. This is leading to a narrowing of the so-called 'digital divide' between large and small.

Less good news for the UK is that the proportion of businesses that allow customers to order online (37 per cent) is significantly below the level of other leading nations. UK businesses trading online are also still trailing leading countries in terms of the average proportion of sales made online, as well as the average proportion of goods and services ordered online.

business processes

The 2004 benchmarking study is a comprehensive report and provides insight into the components that make up the IT or 'e-business' picture. As well as highlighting technology adoption the comparisons between countries include the environments that companies operate in – ie. government regulation, quality of information – and levels of awareness of IT and the extent to which IT supports business processes.

Clearly, such processes differ radically among industry sectors. Service industries such as retail and banking tend to be highly information intensive and therefore IT driven, whereas in manufacturing, for example, there is less emphasis on IT. Trends that show the importance of various technologies to industry sectors are well set out in the annual *European e-Business Report* from the European Commission. The report covers industries such as textiles, electrical, retail and tourism, showing how the relevance of technologies such as Internet connectivity, resource planning and sales and marketing systems varies, and where the potential lies for more investment.

And, according to a report from CIO Connect, a networking organisation for IT managers, businesses simply differ in their readiness to innovate through their use of IT. Some companies, including Tesco, DHL and Easyjet, see it as vital in their aim to stay or become market leaders, while others are more conservative. IT people like using car analogies – do you need a high performance sports car or a delivery van in terms of IT? In a report entitled *Measure for measure: driving IT performance*, CIO Connect looks at the spectrum of IT's alignment with business – from being a high-profile, strategic partner down to a utility provider of a reliable service.

It describes various approaches to measuring IT performance using techniques and tools such as the balanced scorecard and Six Sigma, and also looks closely at benchmarking ideas, such as comparison of IT spend within industries, benchmarking suppliers, and even comparing internal departments. Above all, CIO Connect says it is the quality and skills of people involved in the IT side that determines the ability to support the business.

The fact that even today we are still seeing reports that companies are grappling with IT and business alignment shows that it is a highly complex issue, especially in large organisations, and that cultural or people issues are usually centre stage. There have been numerous texts written about major problems in aligning IT – it's been 20 years since ideas about 'hybrid IT/business managers' were mooted (and largely forgotten), and even now IT managers are excluded from working at board level in many companies.

At last, though, there are signs that the business and technology camps are learning to work together. A recent study by Accenture found that 'the historic tension between business managers and their IT counterparts is diminishing'.

closer co-operation – better productivity

A large proportion of both business and IT managers, for example, believe that IT is under-delivering against investment, says Accenture. The vast majority of both groups also believe that better use of IT has been the principal driver of productivity gains over the past three years.

They are also in broad agreement about the main challenges. Gaining synergies across business units was identified as the most significant challenge by nearly two-thirds of each group. They also acknowledge that there should be more business ownership of IT projects.

The study also found that when business and IT goals are not aligned, IT projects are more likely to fail. For example, nearly one-third of respondents reported IT project failure rates of 41 per cent to 70 per cent – with correspondingly low scores for 'strong' or 'totally aligned' business and IT.

Failure can take many forms – from complete abandonment to less than optimal use. Sometimes IT produces surprises or unintended benefits. But the same principles apply whether it's a major decision support system or a seemingly

AGILITY QUOTIENT

☐ sensing
What systems do you have in place for every employee, at every level, to spot new market or product needs and get that information fast to the decision makers who can make it happen?

☐ strategising
How effective are your problem-solving and planning methods? Are they fast (within 48 hours), practical and used daily at every meeting?

☐ deciding
Is there a formal process in place for making good decisions? Does every manager use it consistently? Can decisions be made at several levels without having to check with a committee or getting group approval?

☐ communicating
Does everyone involved with a change, decision or new strategy know about it (within 24 hours)? Is everyone in the company treated as a key partner in change?

☐ acting
How fast can you bring a new product, service or idea to market? And, how can you do it even faster?

Source: Gartner

simple company website – IT is there to drive the business forward. The 'agility quotient' box above provides a high-level summary of initial questions to ask about your company's fitness in the IT stakes.

Further assistance is available from Oracle, which has created an IT healthcheck to help companies to compare how they are doing, as compared with other companies of a similar size. To access it go to www.oracle.com/start and enter keyword 'success'. The questions contained on the site are also listed in the resource section of this guide (see page 74).

① Preparation: You talk to an HP expert about safeguarding data

② Prevention: You get the world's #1 selling server/storage solution

③ Precaution: You set up the system's one-button disaster recovery

④ Protection: Your system kills a virus, but it was in self-defense

More advice before you buy and more support after.
www.hp.com/smb/dataintegrity

ADVICE	TECHNOLOGY	SUPPORT
With 210,000 certified partners worldwide, there's one nearby to customize a safe data solution for your business.	For outstanding uptime, pair the dependable HP ProLiant ML350 G4 server and its Intel® Xeon™ Processor with the HP StorageWorks DAT 72 tape drive.	One-button disaster recovery brings everything back in one step. HP Care Packs can provide higher levels of uptime and support services.

— HP's Smart Office program: A broad range of hardware, service and support for small and medium businesses. —

strategic IT spending

Businesses needn't spend more – but rather more wisely – on IT, says, David Reynolds, chief executive, IAAITC, the Independent Association of Accountants Information Technology Consultants

According to the DTI's 2004 *International Benchmarking Study*, while 77 per cent of UK businesses have a documented business plan, only 32 per cent of them include IT as an integral part of their business strategy. In fairness to UK businesses, the survey did reveal that of the eight participating countries, the UK and South Korea are both most likely to have a business plan. And, the UK did lead – just ahead of Sweden – with 32 per cent of businesses that have IT as part of the overall business strategy.

But in this case, being top is not good enough, since while another 24 per cent of businesses do also have a documented IT strategy – making a total of 56 per cent – there are still 44 per cent of businesses that have no IT strategy at all.

EXECUTIVE SUMMARY

- too many companies fail to target IT spending effectively
- every IT project needs clearly defined and documented objectives
- the independent perspective of an external consultant can prove invaluable
- before embarking on a project, you should determine how it will affect the business and the level of risk it poses

aimless spending

Given that cost is still regarded as the greatest barrier to successful IT implementation, you cannot help wondering how much of the hundreds of millions invested by this country each year on IT is actually spent with any strategic business objective in mind. One might even go so far as to suggest that probably half of that spend delivers no strategic benefit to the business. A Datamonitor report in 2004 actually showed that the reality is that 80 per cent of all IT budgets is spent simply on standing still.

So, what can we do to improve the situation and spend our money more effectively? We almost certainly do not need to spend more, but just to spend what we do more intelligently.

Unfortunately, far too many IT projects start life as the result of strong departmental champions. The accounts department, for example, decides that they need a new accounting system. Cost justifying the investment to the board will not be a problem for them. The impact that the new system may have on other parts of the business will often be ignored and it will be a brave sales or development director who argues that the money could be better spent on his or her department.

A strong IT director who understands the business will, of course, be able to take a 'helicopter view' of all operations and projects. That said, many of them will be more interested in ensuring that their budget is kept intact and that they can upgrade to this year's latest version of XYZ software, even if most staff still can't use the current version effectively.

clearly defined deliverables

But every IT project – regardless of size – should have a clearly defined, documented set of deliverables. However, defining the deliverables is often easier said than done. Here are some questions to kick start the process:

☐ usually everybody can define the benefits, but what about the downsides, the changes in processes required, the risks?

☐ the benefits are clear, but how will you achieve them?

☐ do you already have the requisite knowledge and skills needed to implement the project successfully or will your staff need training? You need to think about both the implementation of the project and how to continue using it effectively.

- ☐ if you don't have all the skills how will you obtain them, over what period of time and at what cost?

- ☐ what other areas of the business will be impacted? Will any department be adversely affected – even for a short time? Does it matter if they are and, if so, what steps will you take to minimise any potentially negative impacts?

- ☐ having agreed the deliverables with all staff likely to be affected, what criteria will be used to measure the success of the project?

- ☐ how will you measure that the actual deliverables meet your expectations, and over what period?

planning the process

So, now you know what you are trying to achieve. You know what will constitute a successful project, and everybody has bought into those twin objectives. The next step is to plan the process to ensure that it actually happens. There are plenty of books on project management but for most IT projects you probably will not need something as sophisticated as the Prince methodology, which is excellent in its place. (Chapter 3 outlines a specific framework that businesses can use to ensure that a methodical approach is taken and that IT and the business strategy are aligned effectively.)

You do need somebody who actually owns the project and is going to take responsibility for managing the processes both internally and externally (see chapter 7 for more).

This is often where an external project manager or consultant is invaluable. They will be totally focused on the project with no other day-to-day worries to distract them. They will become the communication hub between your staff and your supplier(s) and, more importantly, will have no vested interests within your business or in protecting the supplier.

managing the change

If things are going to have to change as a result of this project – and if not why are you doing it? – then the change process has to be defined and managed as well. Again, it's best to get this established before the project commences. It's all very well giving the finance department the greatest software in the world but if such a move impacts negatively on five other departments it may turn out not to be the best investment you've ever made.

Having clarified what it is you want, you'll probably want it yesterday. However, you need to be realistic in setting a timetable. And, be careful not to choose a supplier on the basis that they're prepared to drop everything else immediately and throw all their resource behind your project. Tempting though this is, it doesn't bode well for a long-term partnership.

Some IT suppliers are very good at 'spinning plates' and can always squeeze one more project in, but even they will reach their limit, beyond which several 'plates' will come crashing down. Make sure your project is not one of them, and try to ensure that you meet as many of your supplier's team before you commit to the project.

determining the level of risk

Finally, you need to identify what the level of risk is? On a small project the risk may be minimal. For example, if you are upgrading 100 users to a new version of a spreadsheet the risk that the spreadsheet will not calculate basic formulas is pretty minimal. If, however, you have users who really know how to stretch a spreadsheet – with built-in macros, look-up tables, database links, etc. – the risk increases of their being some problems in upgrading all existing spreadsheets. On the other hand, if you are a scientific organisation that uses the 20 per cent of spreadsheet functions that the rest of us do not even know exist, there may be a very real risk that the new version of the software does not quite do things the way that all your users expect.

So, when considering risk you have to consider your's, the supplier's, what the probability is and, most importantly, what you can do to mitigate the risk. The point of this exercise is to understand what your risk mitigation action would be in a worst-case scenario. Taking the spreadsheet example above, you would presumably be able to test the software before you committed to the upgrade. Even if having done all the tests you rolled out the new version only to find it didn't actually work, you could always revert to the previous version. So, in the worst-case scenario it is hardly likely to be a business critical issue. Or is it?

key areas of risk management

You can take any IT project and break it down into four key areas of risk management: size; structure; impact; change management.

Consider the size of the project in terms of the number of hours or weeks it will take, the size of the team, the sites affected, and the organisations to coordinate. While it is true that the bigger the project and the more people involved, the harder it is to manage, it is also fair to assume the larger the job, the less likely it's success will depend on one person.

Other important questions to consider are:

- ☐ what is the structure?
- ☐ is the scope well-defined and documented?
- ☐ does everybody know what you are trying to achieve?
- ☐ are the deliverables well-defined and documented?
- ☐ are the benefits quantifiable?
- ☐ how experienced is your team – collectively and individually? What about your suppliers?
- ☐ is this all new, or is there experience and expertise available elsewhere that you can draw on?
- ☐ does everybody understand the impact of this project and how, why and where it supports the business plan?
- ☐ are there any dependencies outside of your control?
- ☐ how will you manage changes to policies and processes?
- ☐ do you need to document them and/or get them agreed?
- ☐ how will you ensure that the quality of the new processes is robust?

could do better

Today, IT is cheaper, more pervasive and more robust than it is has ever been. In the business community, very few of us do not depend on IT to complete our everyday tasks. The UK is, without doubt, one of the leading nations in the effective deployment of IT. Unfortunately, there are still not enough businesses, particularly small and medium ones, doing it properly.

a plan for aligning business and IT

Successfully aligning IT and your business strategy rests on balancing their respective – sometimes disparate – needs, says Colin Beveridge, Guidelines author for the National Computing Centre

EXECUTIVE SUMMARY

- [ ] understanding value chains is key as these represent the relationships between the business functions and the IT estate
- [ ] you need to identify what potential pressures will shape and influence your business in the future
- [ ] successful alignment of IT and business strategy depends on communication, collaboration, mutual trust and understanding
- [ ] the real value of planning is the ability to manage changing circumstances

How can we replace the old-world thinking of 'retro-fitting' business functionality into an IT strategy with a business-focused approach?

The following process addresses these fundamental questions:

- [ ] what have you got now?
- [ ] what do you need for the future?
- [ ] how do you change things to make your visions reality?
- [ ] how do you make sure that IT remains relevant in an evolving business?

Despite the growing trend towards service homogenisation and widespread adoption of packaged software, there are still real opportunities for IT to make a difference. In today's commercial environment the primary objective of a business should be to have robust, but adaptable, technology throughout the organisation, which can facilitate an agile business strategy.

understand the business – identify and document all of your business processes, both formal and informal

The IT function in every business is about capturing, processing, storing and distributing quality business information. So, the first principle of aligning IT with your business strategy is to gain a crystal clear understanding of the business itself. Without such a view, it is impossible to achieve the desired outcome.

A good starting point is to consider the multi-tier nature of your organisation and how it fits into the rest of the business world. Key areas to document include organisation charts, formal and informal processes, markets, products, key customers and suppliers.

acknowledge the culture – analyse the structure, ethos and nature of your organisation

The most frequently overlooked aspect of IT strategy definition is the cultural analysis of the organisation, ie. understanding the way you do things, rather than just what you do. It is important to match the nature of your systems to the nature of your business. If you do not make this connection properly, you will always struggle to achieve optimum performance from your IT investments. You need to examine your culture, and sub-cultures, after which you can consider the appropriate IT culture for each business sub-culture.

know the IT estate – identify and document all IT assets, software applications and delivery channels

Document both the components of the IT estate and how they are aggregated into the company's offerings. You need to collect a wide range of information, from exactly how many assets you have – and their technical attributes – to who manages them, and who pays for them.

discover the value chains – identify and document the touch-points/relationships between the business and the IT estate

Every business consists of various value chains, each of which combines a number of inputs and transforms them to add value before producing an output.

This may be a product or an input for yet another value chain. Such value chains are found in every type of organisation, wherever inputs are transformed into outputs.

By analysing the constitution of your value chains you can discover what is really driving your business/IT activity and so identify the key factors that are crucial to effective strategic planning and alignment. You can do this by documenting the relationship between the business activities and the underlying IT activities/ resources that are aggregated within each value chain.

interpret the context – gather and collate intelligence about influential factors, internal and external

Before you begin planning in earnest, you need to know what pressures will shape and influence the business in the future. This requires gathering intelligence from both internal and external sources, analysing the raw information and determining how any consequent change may affect the existing business functions, culture, IT estate and value chains.

Internal factors will include corporate and business unit plans, maintenance programmes and renewal of infrastructure. External factors are rather more diverse and difficult to capture but will include legislation, economic and customer trends, and skills availability.

determine the change agenda – analyse the context, the business strategy and influential factors; identify impacts and implications for the IT estate

The change agenda consists of parallel paths. At the highest level, these can be expressed under headings that include regulation, corporate policy, business and technology initiatives, and customer-driven and vendor-driven change.

Successfully balancing the sometimes disparate needs of the various change agenda paths is the core feature of IT and business strategy alignment. The IT department and the other business units need to have regular bi-lateral exchanges of information and effective communication. Each party needs to know the other's intentions, in good time, preferably before a definite commitment is made to adopt a change in direction.

the impact of change

To assess the impact of a change, consider its likely effects on IT functions and strategies such as service delivery, security, risk, content management, storage, etc. A disciplined and comprehensive approach to change assessment will both flush out the true financial implications and operational consequences and help to formulate the relative priorities and benefits of potential changes.

set the agenda

Following the change/impact assessment the next step is to strike an appropriate balance between cost, value and priority. This means setting the change agenda according to the likely commercial constraints and the investment cycle.

This is a cyclical process, where you continually need to identify requirements, prioritise timescales and functionality, model and test changes, implement and review. The change agenda defines your options for change, giving you a framework for decision-making and goal setting. What it cannot do, though, is to spell out the details of the journey – for that you need a roadmap.

chart the technology roadmap – prioritise, time-line and optimise the change agenda

The corporate change agenda outlines the nature of the changes that must be applied to the business processes and the IT estate. The technology roadmap takes us a step further by describing in detail how the relevant technology changes will be implemented, with respect to individual systems, time-scales and priorities.

It's important that you have a technology roadmap, rather than working directly from the change agenda, because the systems-centric view of the organisation will always be quite different from the business-centric view.

plan the work programme – translate the technology roadmap into business unit plans

Business units move at different speeds due to commercial, economic or geographic constraints, which means that each one should have its own, dedicated, IT programme of work. This will show when, where and why activity will be taking place. This view not only helps the departments/teams to see how they will be involved/affected by change but it also helps them to make a stronger connection between their business activities and the underlying technology services. The easiest way to do this is to start with a service delivery matrix, showing the take-up of services across the business units.

populate the delivery framework – resource the programme

The delivery framework is the overall programme of work for the delivery of IT in support of all business operations. The framework includes not only items associated with specific projects but also the daily routine operations, ie. the business-as-usual activities. It is absolutely vital to be able to see the entire picture because otherwise it is impossible to understand the real implications of deviating from plans, or deciding how best to meet changing circumstances.

However, you do not need to integrate plans beyond inherent dependencies, as this can create unnecessary complexity and confusion. What is essential though is a work-scheduling tool that underpins the entire delivery framework. Every IT department, regardless of size, has a certain capacity for work, which may be supplemented with external capability, acquired from other providers – either permanently, or on an ad hoc basis.

achieve the business benefit – implement the delivery framework

The ultimate test of the IT alignment will be to see how well you deliver the promises made to internal 'customers'. The main tasks now are as follows:

☐ managing the delivery framework
  The real value of planning derives not only from accurate forecasting but also from the ability to manage changing circumstances. If everything always went exactly as planned we wouldn't need so many managers. Optimise your chances of successful delivery by not making promises you know you can't deliver. Ensure you allocate resources to the most valuable task and carry out impact assessments whenever the delivery framework is challenged.

☐   managing relationships with customers and providers
Certain aspects of our ability to deliver business benefits depend on the active participation and co-operation of customers. We are also increasingly dependent on third-party providers to fulfil our obligations. For successful fulfilment throughout the value chain you need very strong elements of trust between all parties and effective relationship management at every point of contact.

☐   measuring success
Business benefits from IT activity come in many forms, not all of which can be measured in financial terms, at least not directly. Where the introduction of technology is justified largely on the basis of anticipated, notional productivity gains from improved performance, it is up to the initiative sponsor to make sure that the business case is both well-founded and subsequently achieved.

This chapter is an edited version of Aligning IT with Business Strategy, *published by the National Computing Centre (www.ncc.co.uk).*

Big Business Software
Small Business Price

 teamsolve

**Get the power of E-Business Suite Special Edition
from one of these Oracle partners today.**

the goals of an e-business system

> **Many SMEs are being held back by their piecemeal IT systems. Clive Wells, sales consulting manager at Oracle, highlights the benefits of having an integrated approach**

The goals of any commercial IT worth its salt can be summed up as reducing costs, enabling revenue growth and providing effective management information. With e-business trading becoming mainstream and global trading the 'norm',

these goals are intensified as organisations strive for competitive edge. But their remit broadens to encompass new challenges – more efficient electronic collaboration with suppliers, customers and stakeholders; a growing need for regulatory compliance; and flexible business models that adapt quickly to new market opportunities and conditions.

The prevalent IT strategy in the SME sector has been one of piecemeal purchases of 'best of breed' applications using different technologies, from different vendors. These are 'glued' together by interfaces and supplemented by spreadsheets and manual

EXECUTIVE SUMMARY

- ☐ an integrated e-business system will reduce costs, enable revenue growth and provide valuable management information

- ☐ it will also deliver easier and cheaper communications, both within the company and with external partners and suppliers

- ☐ daily business intelligence is available as a standard part of the system, with no additional effort or cost to obtain it

systems. Such an arrangement reflects an absence of IT strategy and is symptomatic of a tactical approach by individual departments in response to their specific needs. This 'patchwork quilt' of systems is usually inefficient to run and costly to maintain, and consequently affects the business's performance and potential.

A good example of this is customer information. If an organisation has separate systems for sales order processing, financial management and customer relationship management, then customer information is contained in all three. If the customer's address changes then it needs to be changed within each system, which encapsulates the issue of disparate systems: whether to update them manually or automate the update. Both require investments in time and/or money to achieve, and an automated solution requires ongoing maintenance as each of the three systems undergoes upgrade over time.

Another serious consequence is that management information about customers' buying patterns, their payment history and the frequency and type of after-sales contact they have with the organisation are all contained in different systems. This makes a complete view of the customer difficult to obtain without spending yet more time and money on creating a data warehouse to combine all three information sources. And this is just one example of the hidden consequences of this patchwork quilt approach to IT. It's no wonder that a recent survey of SME business leaders by industry analyst Datamonitor revealed that the top imperative driving SMEs is the desire to reduce costs to become more competitive.

Yet IT has never before had so much to offer the business community. An IT strategy aligned to a business strategy can contribute significantly to achieving the organisation's objectives. By adopting the enterprise-thinking and associated systems an SME can now implement an affordable and effective e-business infrastructure and realise considerable business benefit from it.

Business strategies are delivered by a set of business processes, and these processes are delivered by systems. It follows that the success of the strategy is directly affected by the quality of the processes and systems employed. As the following sections show, an integrated e-business system is the best way to deliver the quality processes needed for success.

reducing costs to increase competitiveness – process automation

E-business reduces costs by automating as many processes as possible, preferably from start to end. All processes are undertaken within one integrated system, with workflow controlling and managing the process according to business-defined rules. This eliminates interfaces and provides the most efficient route from A to B. Data about customers, suppliers, products, etc. is held once within the e-business system, and is shared and validated automatically, which means optimal efficiency and accuracy.

A good example is the sales order-to-cash process. An order is priced, validated and accepted electronically from multiple sources within the integrated e-business system, such as a web storefront, an agent using customer relationship management, a salesperson using a mobile facility from the field and a traditional order entry office. The booked order is processed automatically by the order-processing module and controlled by workflow, according to business rules. This could include a verification and review stage (if the order is a more complex configuration of a model) or it could be routed directly to stores for issue.

Physical stock transactions and accounting entries for cost of sales, revenue recognition and the customer invoice are generated automatically, with the invoice transmitted electronically to the customer. Not only is manual intervention minimised, the business transactions have been processed and accounted for, all within a single system. This is cost-efficient and accurate and provides timely information for credit control, sales analysis and accounting purposes.

The e-business approach contrasts with that of many SMEs, which operate with multiple systems, typically resulting in inefficiency, inaccuracy and, consequently, higher IT costs and poorer business performance.

enabling revenue growth by improving departmental collaboration and communication

Datamonitor highlighted a second key driver for SMEs – improving departmental collaboration and communications. This is where an integrated e-business system can really score results because Internet technology is all about easier and cheaper communication internally within the company and externally with suppliers and customers. The net effect of this is that electronic trading and information flow is enabled and the latest theories of collaborative supply chains and ERP II can be put into practice. Any organisation, with the right technology infrastructure and an integrated e-business set of applications, can now participate in a supply chain and therefore extend its trading opportunities and work more effectively with its supply chain partners.

Business strategies adapt to conditions and introducing new and effective channels to market requires a system infrastructure to support them. Selecting an e-business system with the right credentials greatly increases the chances of executing a successful strategy. A modular design – one that lets you add additional functionality, such as an online web storefront, a mobile sales or service capability or an interaction centre, while sharing existing processes and data – should be the aim.

After all, why waste all that customer information that's been carefully compiled by your finance and field sales teams when you want to introduce a telephone sales or service operation into the business? And, why waste time and money integrating another business application to support this channel when it will only perpetuate the problems of fragmented data and systems? Choose one that has the options inbuilt, but lets you implement them when you need them.

effective management information

The emphasis here is on effectiveness of information, ie. information that is timely, accurate and relevant. It's fair to say that we are awash with information today. This can make it difficult to see the 'wood' for the 'trees' and to get the right information to support decision making and control the business operationally.

When separate business applications are deployed they all produce information about the activities they support. Hence ledgers produce financial information, sales order processing systems produce sales statistics, etc. However, when business performance information is needed that requires data from several systems, it becomes necessary to build a data warehouse and deal with the issues of data cleansing, replication and inaccuracy. And, it costs time and money to build and maintain.

With an integrated e-business system the information dividends are realised. Daily business intelligence is available as a standard part of the system, with no additional effort or cost to obtain it. The intelligence is part of the system, a by-product

from this...

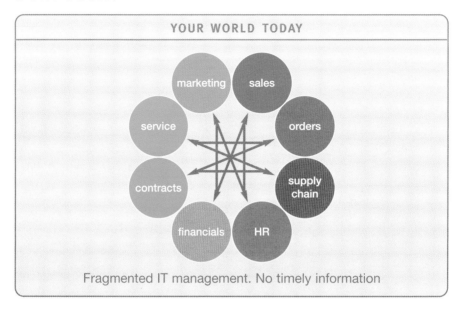

YOUR WORLD TODAY

marketing · sales · orders · supply chain · HR · financials · contracts · service

Fragmented IT management. No timely information

...to this

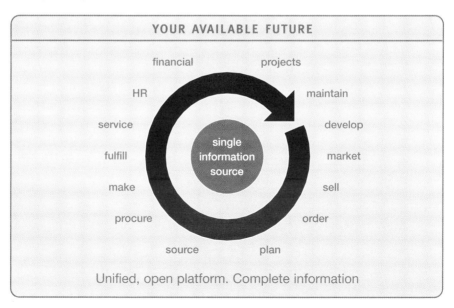

YOUR AVAILABLE FUTURE

financial · projects · HR · maintain · service · develop · fulfill · single information source · market · make · sell · procure · order · source · plan

Unified, open platform. Complete information

of transaction processing. It is timely (produced immediately from the single data source), accurate (it comes directly from the data source, not from a warehouse) and relevant (it produces industry-standard performance metrics). Graphical presentation, with supporting 'drill down', enables trends in performance to be measured, with immediate access to underlying data.

The third SME imperative highlighted by Datamonitor is that of a consistent IT solution across the organisation and this is felt keenly when it comes to management information. So companies often spend a lot of administration effort preparing monthly reports, say, by amalgamating information offline in spreadsheets, because the underlying systems cannot produce it. With an integrated set of applications the process of producing information is streamlined because it is produced directly and automatically from the one system. Consistency of information, in terms of the single set of data being reported on and the presentation of that data, can be used more reliably across the organisation as a basis for informed decision making.

the future

We've briefly discussed the goals of an e-business system and how important it is for a business strategy to have effective systems to deliver it. With most companies planning for growth it is essential to invest in systems and processes that will grow with the organisation and provide it with future options to exploit opportunities with new or revised business models. A single, integrated set of e-business applications offers companies a low-risk IT strategy that aligns with a business strategy by reducing costs, supporting and enabling revenue growth, and can deliver quality management information.

To find out more about Oracle and e-business visit www.oracle.com/start and enter keyword: 'success'.

business software applications

There are a number of core processes that virtually any business carries out. Dennis Jarrett, business and technology writer, advises on maximising their efficiency and effectiveness with the right IT

Business today is increasingly reliant on IT systems – particularly in the key business software application areas of finance, sales and marketing and collaboration. The right solution will be a major asset to a business, with systems that directly impact on strategy as well as more tactical issues of cost-effectiveness. The wrong solution is not only a dangerous drain on precious finances, but can jeopardise competitive advantage.

finance

In the majority of small and medium-sized enterprises, the finance systems are the core of the business. Their efficiency and effectiveness determine whether or not the business can thrive (or, indeed, survive). The paradox is that most conventional finance applications are purely administrative cost centres that, in truth, add no value and contribute no profit.

EXECUTIVE SUMMARY

- [ ] the more effective the integration, the more valuable the information the system will deliver
- [ ] the right system will automate and simplify the whole sales cycle, and help to cut overall costs
- [ ] an integrated approach needs to support the collaboration between internal units and between the business and external parties

The primary requirement of a finance system is to process transactions quickly and efficiently, but it will have additional characteristics that can feed directly into the value chain.

For one, there is a financial impact from everything the business does, and information from all the functional applications within the business ends up in the ledgers one way or another – cost of sales from inventory, invoices from sales order processing, production costs from manufacturing, etc. The ease with which this happens will determine how efficiently information is processed. Business processes should be organised around outcomes, not the component tasks. The same applies to the systems that support those processes. A high level of integration is a feature of the forward-looking enterprise, and this should be designed into the systems rather than bolted on.

The more effective the integration, the more opportunity there is to realise value from information about the business – information that can be used to improve the quality and timeliness of management decisions. All financial systems produce a statutory level of management information if only in the form of simple management accounts. But what's important is that these systems can and should provide true business intelligence – identifying costs, analysing revenue fluctuations, providing useable profitability matrices – from the financial data. For sales orders, for instance, it should be possible to drill down through the financial values back to the supplier detail.

Financial systems should also be sufficiently well organised to help compliance with the standards required by statutory or regulatory bodies. Conformity is often a prerequisite for trading with major customers in government, too. Generating the required proofs and associated documentation will be easier if the appropriate reporting tools are built into the system.

However, at present, the financial managers of many small and medium-sized companies still find themselves dependent on several different systems. Some or all of these will probably be outdated. Many will be unable to exchange information to produce required summaries and analyses. Inevitably, this fragmentation means a lot of rekeying and physical uploading or downloading of data. The result is that, at best, it's challenging to transact daily financial activities with accuracy and efficiency and, at worst, it's difficult or impossible to monitor the daily financial position effectively.

A single integrated financial management system will provide accurate and efficient information management in real-time, with precise reporting on demand

CASE STUDY

The Specialist Schools Trust (SST) is the lead body for the government's specialist schools programme, with a remit to build a network of high-performing secondary schools in partnership with business and the wider community. The Trust employs 200 staff and heads a network of over 2,600 affiliated secondary schools.

Historically, SST expanded very quickly in a short space of time. Consequently, it outgrew its existing systems capabilities, which meant its project-based working methods were not well supported and its purchasing activities were unstructured.

The trust needed new systems that could address its growing financial management and purchasing needs. On the recommendation of Oracle partner PDG Consulting, it selected Oracle's E-Business Suite Special Edition software with pre-configured modules for general ledger, accounts receivable, accounts payable, cash management and purchasing. Additional functionality was provided for Internet accounts and project-based costing.

Since installing the software the trust has significantly enhanced its ability to manage and control its finances:

☐ manual processes have been automated

☐ the reliance on ad-hoc spreadsheets has been eliminated

☐ financial performance can be analysed in ways that were previously impossible

☐ the cost of running the finance function has reduced in relation to the rest of the business

More SME case studies can be found at www.oracle.com/start and enter keyword 'success'.

– exactly what you need for genuine control of the business. It should give you the ability to close accounts rapidly and manage cashflow efficiently combined with the quality of information that allows confident decision-making.

sales and marketing

According to research conducted by Oracle and Datamonitor, increasing sales and market share is one of the top priorities for SMEs. In the face of ever-increasing competition, they are looking for ways to accelerate the sales cycle and maximise every selling opportunity. (For more details of the report, see page 66.)

A relatively small but strategic investment in IT systems can support and enable such aims – though only when implemented as part of a strategic approach that addresses some of the fundamentals of the business.

One of those fundamentals will be the whole sales cycle. The right system will automate and simplify, while helping to reduce overall costs. Where possible, business processes should progress simultaneously rather than in linear fashion – and in sales order processing that is eminently feasible, given a suitable software solution.

For example, an incoming order could automatically and simultaneously progress to accounting – for credit checks, price calculations, invoicing and ledger allocations – to manufacturing – for inventory checks, production, allocation and fulfilment – to CRM – to initiate feedback initiatives and any up-selling or cross-selling options – and so on.

This level of automation means that sales order processing is simplified, and appropriate procedures enforced. Equally important though are the benefits in terms of the customer relationship, which offers the organisation a significant competitive differentiator.

Another business fundamental is the improved visibility and ease of access that results from Internet-based interaction. Sources of sales are becoming more varied, especially with Internet-based procurement. The new economy demands that the company has implemented systems that provide for online sales and order processing. For many, it will be important that customers have enhanced access via the Internet – not just to place orders, but also, for instance, to check stock availability, to track fulfilment or even to pay.

E-invoicing, for example, isn't just about emailing invoices, although that in itself is a major benefit. Removing paper processes means you remove the cost of handling the paper. But e-invoicing is just one visible point of communication between buyer and seller. Both of them will have IT systems for processing the transaction, and e-invoicing means the accounts and procurement systems of all the companies involved can be linked in a supply chain that benefits from lower administrative costs, fewer errors and greater transparency.

The ability to order on-line, by email or by fax can make life easier for the customer and is likely to result in fewer sales drop-outs. Providing communication systems that are available 24/7 and internationally will assist with business efficacy, but it will also improve the relationship with partners, suppliers, and customers.

CASE STUDY

Mark Warner is a specialist independent travel company that offers holiday packages that can be personalised to suit client's requirements. Clients can specify travel preferences, make childcare arrangements and reserve sporting activities and excursions at the time of booking. Some 80 per cent of bookings are made directly through Mark Warner's call centre, with the remaining 20 per cent coming from high street travel agents.

The company's original focus was on summer and ski packages, but it has since diversified to keep up with demand from loyal customers. Its aim is to expand into mid-range and potentially long-haul travel, to offer all year-round products. As a result, the company's IT systems have needed to be revisited. Booking a holiday comprising several different elements was a cumbersome process, that was taking up to 25 minutes. And, the reservations system could not integrate with back-office systems, which made reconciling figures and running ad-hoc queries on bookings data a time-consuming manual task.

The company now has itour, a web-enabled reservations system provided by Oracle partner BlueSky Travel Systems. The solution means packages can be assembled and reservations confirmed within five minutes. Migrating to an integrated, scalable solution also lets Mark Warner run its business according to market demand. Subsequently, the company has been able to introduce multiple channels to market, increase salesforce productivity, boost customer loyalty and diversify its product offering.

More SME case studies can be found at www.oracle.com/start and enter keyword 'success'.

The integrated approach also offers ready availability of sound and usable management information. It can facilitate, for example, seeing where and how the marketing budget is being spent, and in assessing the results. At the strategic level this will include analysis of customers, products and marketing performance. If customer and sales intelligence from all the different sources and interactions is brought together, you can manage leads and opportunities to focus on the high-margin options.

collaboration

Collaboration is an essential element of the systems that support a forward-looking business. It is a useful option, since it fits the logical strategic goal of maximising productivity from existing investment and employees.

As a policy, collaboration applies both to internal and external issues. Lack of internal collaboration affects businesses of all sizes, but larger organisations often have sufficient resources and reserves to cope. The challenges can be greater for the smaller enterprise. You can see it at work in departmental demarcations: manufacturing doesn't get an accurate picture of demand from sales and marketing, purchasing doesn't get a clear view of manufacturing requirements, sales and distribution aren't updating inventory and no-one is keeping finance up-to-date with current status and future transaction activity.

An integrated, collaborative solution means that a transaction initiated by one department will automatically feed into all other relevant systems. In addition, management can call for reports – real-time on-demand reports – to provide anything from a snapshot of the whole business to progress on an individual order. This can give a company improved business efficiency and a confident approach to decision-making.

Outside the organisation, the collaborative approach can be even more attractive – not just as a means of reducing costs, but as a positive approach to increasing revenue and profitability. The system can deliver improved customer service and enhanced relationships with suppliers.

In part those benefits flow from the ability to provide the customer with more accurate and faster information for enquiries, orders, status tracking and other interactions. The best solutions will give the customers secure online 24/7 access to your systems, allowing them, for instance, to check inventory or product specifications on a privileged basis.

The availability of timely information on demand also makes a serious customer relationship management function possible – even for the smaller organisation. You can treat customers as strategic partners, providing proactive information and services with specific opportunities highlighted.

The outcome should be more business for minimal investment in marketing. More importantly, though, building and maintaining relationships like this is critical for competitive advantage. If you cannot offer this approach, you can be sure your competitors will.

Similarly, if your suppliers are not able to get accurate forecasting information or regular reports on how well they are serving your business, you will probably find that you do not receive the best possible service from them – and you

CASE STUDY

Hugh Symons Group has more than 30 years' experience in delivering a wide range of IT solutions to customers through an independent reseller network. The company, which has 400 employees and annual revenues of £120m, is based in the UK but also has operations in the US, Australia, South Africa and Singapore.

As the company grew, it became clear that there was a need to replace disparate, unconnected legacy systems with an integrated solution. It chose an 'e-business suite' provided by Oracle partner Inatech that consolidated its four divisions into a single organisation and provided managers with a real-time view of performance.

Decision-makers can now access reports at the desktop in seconds, a process that used to take several hours and require assistance from IT staff. Leveraging corporate data across the company helps improve business intelligence and drive additional sales.

Closer collaboration at every stage of the supply chain – from manufacturer to retailer and end user – is cutting costs and boosting customer service. Hugh Symons has been able to cut stock levels by 10 per cent through more efficient management of its inventory warehouse. Commissions from network providers and resellers are now remitted 50 per cent faster, with less manual intervention required. Internet sales from channel partners are increasing and the company predicts online orders will eventually be a major representation of their orders.

More SME case studies can be found at www.oracle.com/start and enter keyword 'success'.

probably won't get their best prices either. This kind of supply chain integration is increasingly essential to business, both for cost reduction and simply because many suppliers and contractors now demand it.

A business that offers to integrate its systems with those of its customers and suppliers will enjoy the following advantages:

- ☐ strategic importance is increased

- ☐ stock levels are reduced

- ☐ sales are processed more quickly

- ☐ accounts are closed sooner

- ☐ administration is simplified

- ☐ a high level of confidence for all parties is maintained

SOONER OR LATER YOUR BUSINESS WILL NEED A SERIOUS NETWORK. The good news is, you don't need to be a large corporation to have one. Cisco has created a suite of networking products and support services that can be tailored to your way of working. So your business systems can become more automated, more intelligent and more secure. We took a fresh look at everything. Equipment. Appliances. Financing. Support. We designed it all to be easier to understand, easier to implement and most of all, easier to deliver new savings. You may even be able to take that well-deserved holiday.

See what Cisco can do for you. Call **00800 9999 0522** or visit **cisco.com/uk/seriousbusiness** and when you register, you'll receive a free subscription to IQ magazine, the Cisco publication that focuses on Information Technology for today's business.

THIS IS THE POWER OF THE NETWORK. now.

1999_QUIT BOARD TO START UP BUSINESS.

2001_TAKE ON FIRST CORPORATE CLIENT.

2002_MOVE INTO BIGGER PREMISES.

2003_DELEGATE WORKLOAD WITH NEW CISCO NETWORK.

2005_TAKE FIRST HOLIDAY IN FIVE YEARS.

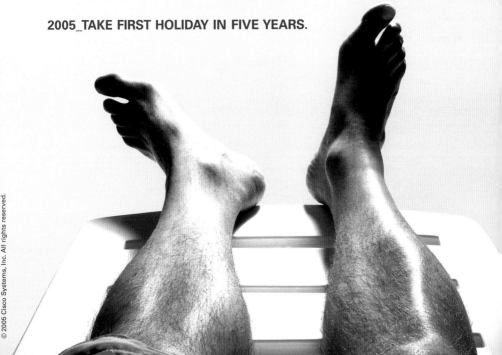

e-commerce

Now the hype is over, e-commerce is helping to boost profits by increasing sales, improving customer retention and reducing costs, says Rod Newing, business and technology writer

As far back as 1998, Tony Blair set out to make the UK the best environment in the world for e-commerce – the subset of e-business that involves Internet transactions. Then, in March 2000, the European summit in Lisbon set the goal of the EU becoming the world's most competitive and dynamic knowledge-based economy. The resulting eEurope Action Plan has the overall goal of exploiting the full potential of the Internet to promote a competitive economy.

In 2000 the dotcom boom was replaced by the dotcom bust. Now that the hype has disappeared, we have seen a steady growth in e-commerce. Organisations are now using the Internet to increase profits by boosting sales, improving customer retention and reducing costs. They are dealing electronically with consumers, with other businesses and with the government.

EXECUTIVE SUMMARY

- [ ] Internet shopping is now overtaking mail order
- [ ] 40 per cent of e-commerce businesses are online-only start-ups
- [ ] in the UK, the huge uptake in broadband access to the Internet is boosting e-commerce
- [ ] not all products sell well over the Internet

there's a lot of it about

An independent Internet World exhibition survey showed that the number of visitors engaged in e-commerce has grown from 18 per cent in 2004 to 52 per cent in 2005. And, research from Actinic carried out among businesses with fewer than 250 employees, showed that e-commerce adoption has risen from 27 per cent of websites in 2003 to 42 per cent in 2004, although this is still only three per cent of all companies.

Interestingly, 40 per cent of e-commerce businesses are online-only start-ups and 75 per cent of e-commerce sites are run by companies with 10 employees or fewer. Most importantly, 72 per cent of retail websites are profitable compared with 53 per cent last year.

business-to-business

Increasingly, large businesses are extending their business processes throughout their supply chain by integrating their systems over the Internet with those of their suppliers and customers. This reduces costs and allows the entire supply chain to react more quickly to changes in consumer demand.

These large companies draw smaller companies into electronic trading. As well as handling the supply chain, this close electronic relationship is allowing different companies to collaborate on a wide range of issues, including marketing or merchandise promotion planning and new product development.

The Internet World research showed that the main benefit of e-commerce is greater efficiency (31 per cent). This was followed by a broader client base (26 per cent), increased turnover (26 per cent), reduced costs (22 per cent), increased profits (22 per cent) and more international business (19 per cent). BT is predicting that by 2007 the UK economy could be boosted by up to £7.5bn through productivity gains attributed to the use of broadband.

broadband consumers

UK businesses can offer suitable products to over a billion people around the world who now have access to the Internet. The rapid uptake of fixed broadband Internet access in the UK is providing a massive catalyst for e-commerce.

According to the government's Office of Communication (Ofcom), there were more than six million fixed broadband connections at the end of 2004. It is now one of the fastest growing consumer products of all time, with a higher take up rate than televisions, CD players, video recorders or mobile phones. By mid-2005 more than 99.6 per cent of UK homes and businesses will be connected to broadband-enabled exchanges – ahead of any other G7 country.

WHICH PRODUCTS SELL WELL?

categories of successful products	examples
digital products	music, software, insurance, bank accounts, shares
those that don't need to be seen or can be bought on price or specification	computers, consumer electronics, books, CDs
mail order products	household goods, stationery
information intensive products	travel
products that appeal to enthusiasts and collectors	cooking supplies, sports memorabilia, out-of-print books and records
frequently purchased commodity items	spare parts, office supplies
categories of less successful products	**examples**
services that focus on a local market	public houses, launderettes, hair salons
items that need to be felt or fitted	fashion

BT connected its five millionth wholesale broadband customer in April 2005, a year ahead of schedule, having connected its last million customers in just four months. It is predicting that by 2007, over 18m people will be shopping online.

Mintel reports that last year Internet shopping overtook mail order in the UK. In 2004, 32 per cent of adults had bought products via the Internet in the previous 12 months, up from just nine per cent in 2000. UK sales per capita for Internet shopping in 2003 were 81 Euros, a close second to Austria.

Wireless broadband is set to provide even more stimulus, as usage of third generation mobile networks and WiFi hot spots increases. This will shortly be joined by WiMax, a much more powerful version of WiFi. As well as notebook computers, mobile commerce will be conducted using personal digital assistants and mobile telephones with Internet connections, known as smartphones.

securing the sale

Some products sell well over the Internet and others are less successful (see box above). The first step is to determine if your product or service is likely to do well online. It is essential to offer a high level of service, so organisations must prepare themselves internally to support the additional online sales. Plans must be drawn up for activities such as handling customer email inquiries, updating inventories on the website, adding new products and deleting old ones, constantly enhancing site security, ensuring smooth delivery and automating outgoing customer communications on order status.

When looking for technology to support e-commerce, several approaches are available:

- [ ] off-the-shelf packages provide a template-driven environment with a degree of customisation. A separate merchant account must be set up for payment

- [ ] integrated packages include a merchant account and transaction processing facility

- [ ] virtual stores are a web-based system that are configured over the Internet

- [ ] business software providers that offer integrated online store modules

eGovernment

Under the eEurope Action Plan, access to all government services must eventually be available online. For businesses, this means the opportunity to submit a range of government forms electronically over the Internet. These include Pay As You Earn (PAYE), self-assessment, value added tax (VAT), corporation tax and company information.

It is anticipated that over the coming years, some government departments may make online returns and reporting compulsory.

E-COMMERCE

Although returns can be completed online, many business software packages provide automated links. This means that forms can be automatically generated and then automatically filed with the government.

Online services are secure, convenient and quick, and they give immediate confirmation of receipt. PMP Research recently found that 24 per cent of companies have already begun e-filing and another 14 per cent intend to do so shortly.

Public sector organisations are increasingly using e-procurement in order to boost efficiency. This can involve using electronic methods for advertising opportunities, evaluating tenders, paying suppliers and managing contracts. E-procurement can benefit suppliers by reducing paperwork, improving efficiency, processing orders more quickly and speeding up payment.

an investment, not a cost

The enabling of a website for e-commerce should not be seen as a cost to the business, but rather as an investment with an attractive return. It allows the organisation to develop close electronic relationships with consumers, other businesses and governments. With the hype out of the way, the serious business of making money on the Internet is well under way.

Solving Datacentre Challenges
Calls for Sharp Thinking…

Many Challenges:
Tightening Budgets, Restricted Space, Limited Resources
Management of Power, Cabling & Cooling

Single Solution:
Dell's PowerEdge™ 1855 Blade Server

And here it is! Dell's PowerEdge 1855 Blade Server delivers new levels of server density and cuts the complexity of cabling by 70%. With powerful performance, 13% more power and thermal efficiency than a conventional 1U rack, and integrated switching for high-speed connections to your SAN or Gigabit Ethernet networks, you may also be surprised to know that after there are more than 5 blades in a chassis, it becomes less expensive to deploy than a 1U rack server*. What's more it's easier to deploy and even re-purpose, thanks to the powerful management tools. Dell's PowerEdge Blade Servers cut your data centre challenges down to size.

Find out more today!
To register for one of our blade workshops, or to find out more about blades
and how to build a scaleable enterprise then please visit www.dell.co.uk/blades

Easy as **D∕ELL**™

delivering a return on investment

> The key to securing a return on your investment is to implement a proper plan and monitor progress against specified targets, says Charles Kavazy, director of IT Services at Hawsons Chartered Accountants

When accounting and administration were first computerised it was obvious that this new way of working would save a significant amount of time. Today, IT impacts on almost every aspect of business and there are numerous IT choices available. Such choices are no longer about clear-cut investments, as business issues and the interaction of people and IT have become far more sophisticated. IT affects not just administration but also key areas such as customer service.

Distinguishing between the relative merits of various IT spending options can be difficult, particularly since many of the benefits are intangible. In addition, IT expenditure is a significant cost for many businesses today and there are a number of research studies that have suggested they don't always get the return on investment (ROI) they should.

EXECUTIVE SUMMARY

- when carrying out an ROI calculation, be practical
- achievement targets should be set within a timetable
- progress should be monitored towards the targets to ensure ROI objectives are achieved
- IT procurement needs to be managed. Once the investment has been made, ensure that you manage your IT staffing, support and training

Of even more interest, IT cost benchmarking studies that were undertaken across companies of a similar size in the same industry found that, in some cases, the highest IT spenders were spending two and even three times more than the lowest spenders. And, the highest spenders were often the least profitable.

So, it is important to:

☐ calculate the ROI

☐ plan to achieve the return

☐ monitor progress to ensure you actually achieve the return

the basic formula

Calculating the return on investment for IT projects is the same as for other investments. ROI is the net increase in gains/benefits divided by the cost of investment and expressed as a percentage. Hence the calculation is:

$$\text{ROI} = \frac{\text{net gains/benefits} \times 100}{\text{cost of investment}}$$

The net gains/benefits are the savings and improvements relating to the investment as a result of carrying out the project. It is important to remember that ROI in IT will be obtained over a number of years, so it cannot be measured over just one year. A more realistic timeframe is three or five years, depending on the project.

There are a number of variants of the formula above but they effectively amount to the same calculation (see page 75 in the resources section for a worked example). You should include all costs that are directly attributable to the project and a relevant proportion of those partially attributable to it.

costs to include

You need to include the following costs:

☐ hardware, including the cost of maintenance

☐ software, including support costs

☐ staff costs, including the relevant cost of internal IT personnel

☐ training, including all your training costs and associated expenses

☐ other costs arising from the investment, such as consultants' fees

calculating net gains

Those benefits that are tangible are easy to measure. For example, cost savings through increased staff efficiencies, such as eliminating duplicated work through the re-keying of data into spreadsheets. However, it is not always easy to calculate such efficiencies across a group of people. Other items that are relatively straightforward to measure include the gains from reduced internal and external IT costs, for example, as a result of replacing legacy systems.

Then there are the intangible benefits such as increased customer satisfaction and reduced delivery times, and indirect benefits, such as the increase in spend per customer as a result of having more sophisticated software that prompts salespeople to offer customers related items. Again, this kind of benefit is tricky to measure because who's to say whether or not the customer was going to buy the complementary product anyway?

The way to resolve this is to make estimates of the cost savings and to be as prudent and practical as possible. Remember that because the calculation includes estimates it can only ever be a guide to help you make your decision.

Different people in an organisation will place different values on the estimate of benefits, often so as to prove or disprove the theory that the IT investment in question is good or bad, dependent on each individual's 'gut feeling'.

Using an ROI calculation is not without flaws. One problem is that there are just too many estimates required. Another is that ROI takes no account of the risk of the investment. Also, depending on how many years you calculate the ROI, you will get a different answer.

Other measures that are used include payback period – the time taken for the investment to pay for itself – discounted cash flow (DCF), net present value (NPV) and total cost of ownership (TCO). Each has its advantages and disadvantages, but the key thing to remember with return on IT investments is that you are in effect trying to predict the future. This means that you do have to use estimates and judgement. So, once you've done your calculations, used your judgement and made the investment, the key step is to plan to obtain the returns you set out to achieve.

And, finally, you must also consider what other factors might impact on the success of the project and hence the return on investment. Ask yourself whether you have the necessary skills and time within your organisation to carry out the project. If not, you should get help from an external consultant. You should also consider the culture of your organisation since it is important not to make too big a change in IT in one go since your staff may find it difficult. And, if you are using a third-party supplier you need to undertake a thorough due diligence check on the products and the supplier.

planning is the key to success

Once you feel ready to go ahead with the investment, the key to delivering your return is to go through the ROI justification and break the project down into targets/achievements and then set milestone dates for each one. So, for example, if you want to make labour savings, put them into the timetable – describing exactly what they are – and then make sure they happen. Progress towards achieving the targets needs to be monitored regularly and carried out at senior management level. The findings should also be reported to the board of directors on a regular basis.

Failure to implement a plan for achieving your targets leads to inefficiency and wasted investment. In one case, a company bought software that included functionality it didn't get round to implementing. Five years later, and after a number of staff changes, everyone had forgotten about the functionality so it still hadn't been implemented. In such cases the scenario can get even worse because the company then buys more software because it assumes the existing software doesn't have the required functionality – even though it does.

practical tips

If you are going to get a return on investment you need to ensure you have a good approach to IT in the areas of:

- ☐ IT procurement
- ☐ IT support and staffing
- ☐ IT training

With IT procurement you should:

- ☐ ensure IT decisions are based on helping to achieve the targets specified in your business plan

- ☐ look at your work processes and procedures before investing in new software as you may be able to do things differently and better. Your current software may have led to inefficient working practices, so be open to new procedures and potential efficiencies offered by the new software

- ☐ have an appropriate level of integration between your systems. If you have disparate software packages check how much it is costing a year to integrate

- ☐ choose an appropriate replacement cycle for hardware

- ☐ be prepared to accept when you've made a wrong decision with IT. Sometimes it can be more costly to continue supporting bad decisions and choices than to replace the systems with what you really need

- ☐ employ IT staff who also understand business and, in particular, your business. This will ensure that you have a business needs focus to IT

- ☐ make sure you maximise your buying power with your IT suppliers. Know your IT costs, review them regularly, and get competitive quotes

With IT support and staffing you should:

- ☐ ensure you don't pay for support more than once. Some companies pay twice or even three times over. First they pay a third party, then they pay an IT manager who tries to solve the problem and finally their users spend too long trying to resolve problems themselves before contacting the supplier

- ☐ consider outsourcing as much IT support as possible since this can yield significant savings

- ☐ create a culture of 'balanced user self help' to avoid users asking the IT department to solve the simplest of everyday IT problems. This will mean that your IT staff can get on with the work they really should be doing without constant distraction

With IT training you should:

- ☐ carry out a training needs analysis and ensure you have an appropriate training plan for each member of staff

- ☐ ensure that staff are trained in what they need to know in the depth they need to know it. It is all too easy for trainers to spend too long on the 'easy stuff' and not enough time on the more difficult stuff or to spend time on functionality staff members won't use

- ☐ use onsite on-the-job training wherever possible, so that staff are trained in what they need to know, in the context in which they need to know it

- ☐ ensure training is carried out just before staff are going to use the functionality to avoid people forgetting what they've been taught

- ☐ ensure new starters are trained adequately and remember that when staff resign, a lot of knowledge about using the software goes with them

To find out more about Hawsons Chartered Accountants, visit: www.hawsons.co.uk

funding options

> **There is a wide range of options available to fund IT, ensuring that organisations remain competitive, says Rod Newing, business and technology writer**

Despite falling hardware prices, most organisations invest considerable sums in building and maintaining their IT infrastructure. Fortunately, the number of options available for financing hardware, software, services and training is growing.

your friendly bank manager

Most mature businesses use bank loans or overdrafts to pay for their computing needs. Overdrafts are best for providing short-term working capital associated with seasonal volatility. Bank loans are more appropriate for purchasing hardware that will last for three to five years, so the term of the loan can be matched to the life of the hardware. Interest rates may be slightly lower.

Another option appropriate for computer and telecommunications equipment is leasing. The bank owns the hardware, but the business is responsible for service, repairs, insurance and physical security.

With a financing lease, payments are calculated to recover the entire cost of the equipment. When it is sold the proceeds are passed back to the customer as a rebate. Operating leases recover the loss in value of the equipment, with the

EXECUTIVE SUMMARY

- [ ] funding should be matched to the life of the equipment, which will have little residual value
- [ ] commercial funding is available through shares, bank loans, leasing and hire purchase
- [ ] major hardware and software vendors have their own financing schemes
- [ ] IT infrastructure is starting to be charged on usage, just like any other utility
- [ ] there are over 2,500 grant schemes that pay out over £5bn a year

bank keeping the proceeds of sale. In the case of computer equipment – which has little residual value – there may not be much difference between the two.

Hire purchase is sometimes used for individual items of computer equipment. Equipment is rented for an agreed period and then purchased outright for a small sum at the end. It works best where the business wants to own an asset at the end, but computer equipment is likely to be obsolete at the end of the term.

start-ups

Many new businesses pay for their initial IT infrastructure with cash raised from venture capitalists through the issue of shares. As the business expands and needs to invest more in product development, buildings, people and equipment, it will issue further shares to existing shareholders. These new funds will cover the cost of upgrading and expanding their computing infrastructure.

vendors

Major IT vendors need to make it easy for their customers to buy their products. Many of them have subsidiaries that provide financing, such as Cisco Capital, HP Financial Services, IBM Global Financing and Oracle Financing. The finance available will include leasing and 'soft' loans that offer low interest rates and easy repayment terms.

Such an arrangement will include the vendor's own hardware, software and services. However, it may also include third-party costs, making it suitable for financing entire projects. These financing schemes are mainly aimed at smaller and medium-sized companies and are available through IT vendors' resellers.

Vendors like to help their customers' businesses grow and stay competitive, and to offer protection against obsolescence. Their leasing plans encourage clients to keep their IT infrastructure up-to-date by returning the old equipment at the end of the term and then leasing the newest technology from them.

Computer rental companies provide low-end personal computers, servers and other equipment. They are excellent for meeting unexpected requirements or known peaks in requirements, but are less attractive as a permanent solution. Some software vendors will also rent out their software.

utility computing

Companies such as Hewlett-Packard and IBM offer outsourcing. This involves purchasing the organisation's complete IT infrastructure and taking over its IT staff. They then manage the dedicated infrastructure on the customer's own premises.

The latest trend is to rent use of a shared external infrastructure. This is known as 'application service provision', 'utility computing', 'software as a service', or 'on-demand computing'.

Instead of having its own infrastructure on its premises, the organisation accesses a third-party provider's infrastructure across the Internet, such as Oracle's On Demand service. At the moment, the hardware and software tends to be dedicated, but eventually many organisations will share a single copy of the software running on a set of servers. Sharing the infrastructure should bring considerable cost reductions through economies of scale.

Just like gas, electricity or water, the company pays only for its usage, calculated as a monthly fee per user. The user organisation saves costs and has more flexibility. It also has access to a higher quality and better managed infrastructure, with higher skills, than it could afford itself.

Utility computing is a natural choice for new organisations setting up businesses from scratch. However, it is a major change for existing organisations that already have their own infrastructure. Any change is most likely to be made when a major upgrade is required.

'free' software

Another way to reduce the financing burden of IT is to use open source software, such as Linux, the UNIX-like operating system. This can be downloaded from the Internet and used free of charge.

In practice, businesses will only use a version of the software for which a commercial support contract is available from companies such as IBM, Novell, Red Hat and their partners. This effectively means that the organisation pays a subscription to use the software.

Some organisations replace old proprietary hardware and operating systems with cheap industry-standard servers running Linux. The cost is usually much less than the maintenance charge that they were paying on the proprietary equipment.

grants

New and growing businesses create jobs and bring wealth. Governments want to encourage and develop trade and commerce, so they assist them with funding through grants. A grant is a form of financial assistance that is not repayable. It is usually a one-off payment to cover a proportion of the costs of a specific project, typically 50 per cent. The Business Link grants and support directory database lists 2,662 separate schemes, which are estimated to pay out £5bn per annum.

In the UK national government funds are available from Westminster, the Scottish Parliament, the Welsh Assembly and the Northern Ireland Assembly, which together control over 100 grant-providing bodies. Local grant providers include Business Link, Small Business Service, Enterprise Agencies, Training and Enterprise Councils, Local Enterprise Companies, Business Connect, Enterprise Trusts, County Enterprise Boards, Scottish Enterprise and Highlands & Islands Enterprise.

The European Commission administers a wide variety of schemes through its Structural Funds and individual Directorates. However, recent research shows that 55 per cent of SMEs are currently unaware that they qualify for EU funding assistance. For details about EU funding programmes see WelcomEurope (www.welcomeurope.com), the UK Euro Info Centre (www.euro-info.org.uk) and SME TechWeb (http://sme.cordis.lu).

A number of schemes are available for small and medium-sized businesses toward the cost of connection and use of broadband. Details are available from BT (www.btbroadbandoffice.com/broadband).

conclusion

There are a wide range of funding options available and most of them are more appropriate than the traditional overdraft. Choosing the right option will reduce costs and provide more flexibility, helping the organisation to stay competitive.

getting your IT contract right

To avoid trouble later on, make sure you get the right advice from a lawyer who specialises in computer law, says Jeremy Holt, head of the Computer Law Group of Clark Holt, Commercial Solicitors

Pity the unfortunate manager. It has been bad enough trying to get the whole IT project organised. Now, possibly at the last moment, the contract(s) have arrived, some with print small enough to make you go blind. You suspect (rightly) that these contracts are one sided in favour of the supplier, but know that the project will only proceed if those contracts are signed. How do you work out what needs to be done, and from who advice can be obtained? This chapter provides a practical framework for dealing with this situation.

EXECUTIVE SUMMARY

- [ ] any IT system will involve buying hardware, software and services
- [ ] hardware is usually the least contentious and often the last component to be chosen
- [ ] there are two types of hardware maintenance – preventive and corrective
- [ ] always ensure that your supplier either owns the copyright to the software or has the right to sublicense it to you

who are you going to call?

You are not going to be able to do this all on your own. You're going to need professional advice, even if it requires tangling with the dreaded lawyers. This means instructing the right lawyers, not necessarily the ones that you normally use, since computer law is a specialist area. The function of a good lawyer is to assess and reduce risk, so in this sense they are a branch of the insurance industry.

To find a decent computer lawyer there are two directories that you might consult: the *Chambers Guide to the Legal Profession* and the *Legal 500*. New versions are published each year. Each has sections on lawyers who specialise in computer law (sometimes called information technology law). These two books can generally be found in the reference section of public libraries. Alternatively, you can ring the Law Society (020 7242 1222) or the Society for Computers and Law (0117 923 7393) for suggestions of lawyers who work in this field and who could help you.

Any computer system will require the purchase of hardware, software and services. When computers first came out the emphasis was very much on the hardware, which in those days was comparatively unreliable. Nowadays the emphasis is much more on the software and services. It is normal to decide on the software first and then to choose the appropriate hardware.

contracts for hardware purchase

Because computer hardware is so much more reliable than it used to be, contracts for the supply of hardware are not generally contentious.

However, the following points must be agreed in detail within a hardware purchase contract: a detailed description of the hardware, a warranty about the quality of hardware, delivery dates, price, acceptance testing, future maintenance and training.

Problem areas that can arise are:

☐ whether the hardware is large enough for anticipated demand in the future

☐ the integration of one kind of hardware with other hardware that may have been supplied by a different vendor

contracts for hardware maintenance

Hardware maintenance is more of a commodity than software maintenance. There are likely to be more alternative suppliers for the maintenance of hardware. Software, by contrast, requires an insight into the way it was originally written.

There are two different types of hardware maintenance – preventive maintenance and corrective maintenance. Preventive maintenance covers the regular testing of the hardware before any problem is reported. Corrective maintenance deals with faults as and when they arise, normally in response to a service call from the customer.

With corrective maintenance the key element is the response time – how quickly will the supplier start to respond to the problem once it is reported? This is generally within a fixed number of working hours – say, eight. This means that an engineer will arrive at the site no more than eight working hours after the problem has been reported to the supplier. It does not mean that the engineer will solve the problem within eight hours – merely that a start will be made to try and solve it.

Payment for hardware maintenance is generally made in advance on either a monthly or quarterly basis. The annual amount varies but is often between 10 per cent and 15 per cent of the list price of the hardware.

contracts for software licences

To put it at its simplest, any contract for software should allow you to use it in the way that you envisaged without the risk that anyone can come along later and say either that you cannot use it any more or that you have got to pay more money.

It follows that one of the first checks that you should do is to confirm that the software supplier either owns the copyright in the software or has the right to sublicense it to you. It is a feature of the computer industry that most software is licensed to end-users by organisations other than the actual owner, ie. it is sublicensed. You should not put up with any oblique answers to your demand to the supplier for evidence that they can license the software to you. They should be able to produce it for you immediately.

contracts for software maintenance

No software of any complexity is ever free from errors. The older the system, the more likely that it will need maintenance. If a system is installed in a rush, it is likely not to have been tested properly and therefore will require more attention post-installation. In some ways future charges for maintenance are the icing on the cake for software developers. If they can generate sufficiently wide sales of the software then support fees can be guaranteed for years to come. It's important for managers to be aware of this as up to three quarters of their software budget may be needed for future software maintenance.

Maintenance or support will normally cover the investigation by the supplier of errors in the system reported by the customer as well as updated documentation, telephone or, more frequently nowadays, online advice. In most cases it will also cover updates of the software. You may want to categorise different kinds of problems into those that could be critical for your business and those that are no more than an irritation to be dealt with next time a new version of the software comes out. The supplier's response time will be different depending on the severity of the problem. The supplier will not normally commit to a fix within a particular period – only that they will start to fix it within a particular time.

One way to avoid maintenance charges from rocketing is to tie them to a percentage of the list price of the software, say 10-15 per cent (although the supplier obviously has control over such list prices).

Payment is almost invariably made in advance. In the past it was for a whole year but now it is more commonly paid three months or a month in advance.

It is also a good idea for the customer to ask the supplier to commit on its part to supply maintenance for the potential life of the software.

essential points about computer contracts

know what you want

Make sure you know exactly what you want and what is achievable, because if you don't know, you're not going to get the contract right

get it in writing

If a particular point is important to you make sure that you get it in writing from the supplier. It may well be that one aspect that is critical to you is not dealt with in the supplier's draft contract at all. If so, get a written acknowledgement of the requirement from the supplier. An ordinary letter from the supplier is sufficient provided that it is either cross-referred to in the main contract or included as a schedule. If the supplier drags its heels and refuses to confirm a point in writing, you should write saying that you are only entering into the main contract on the basis that this point is agreed. If the matter ever goes to court the production of your letter saying this will bring tears of sadness to the supplier's lawyer and tears of joy – well almost – to your lawyer.

decide on support and maintenance

Make sure that you get the supplier to agree to supply support and maintenance for the products purchased for a sensible length of time. You do not want the supplier cancelling support after a couple of years just when your new system is working well. Note that you do not have to commit to take the support and maintenance – ideally your commitment should be on a year-by-year basis.

get adequate training

Make sure that you order enough training. One of the most common reasons for the failure of a computer project is inadequate training. As a rule of thumb, roughly 20 per cent of a project's cost should be spent on training. If it is substantially less than that you should ask why.

secure software source codes

Make sure that you can get access to the source code of the software programs supplied to avoid problems in the future should the supplier either go into liquidation or stop supporting the software. Ideally, the source code should be deposited with an independent third party and kept updated by the supplier as each new version comes out.

Finally, never forget that the contract is a delivery mechanism for ensuring that a project is completed in the right way, at the right time, by the right person and for the right price. No more, no less.

To find out more about Clark Holt, visit www.clarkholt.com

essential sources of information

There is a wealth of online advice and support available to UK businesses involved in developing their IT and communications capability, says Marc Beishon, business and technology writer

Where can businesses go to gain information and advice about their IT and communications capability? The availability and quality of such information is a core differentiator among countries, and the UK is probably better served than most at present.

Websites for all the organisations mentioned under the following headings can be found in the resources section at the end of this guide. For more sources of information see also the recent Director's Guides to mobile working, wireless computing and security.

EXECUTIVE SUMMARY

- there are various government bodies whose websites offer support and guidance on IT for business

- free advice and information is available from a number of independent sources

- the quality of advice from major vendors has greatly improved

government

Government sources of information about IT for business have improved greatly in recent years in line with the emphasis being placed on the UK as a leading 'e-business' player.

The primary source is the Department of Trade Industry (DTI), which has brought together a comprehensive set of practical business guidelines in its 'Achieving best practice in your business' part of its website. There is a communications and IT subsection that includes guides and case studies on the Internet, wireless and mobile, security, integration of systems and processes, and voice and conferencing technologies. Guides of particular interest are on e-business best practice, integrating back office and online systems, and improving relations with customers and suppliers.

In addition, there is guidance on support packages (such as funding and benchmarking); a technology route map; regional e-business clubs; and registration for a monthly newsletter that also gives access to a suite of tools, including a technology benchmarker, an e-business planner and a broadband business service checker.

A lot of new material has been added to the 'Best practice' website in recent months and it is well worth checking on a regular basis.

Complementary to the DTI's site is Business Link, which has a section on IT and e-commerce. This has a set of basic guides to IT topics, such as computerising a business and using technology to do business in new ways. There are also sections on choosing suppliers, how to find an accredited IT consultant, doing business online (including online filing), and events.

Other government sites to note are:

- ☐ Technology means business (TMB)
  An accreditation agency for consultants and companies providing IT information to SMEs. Its site includes case studies and a location service for finding technology advisers. A new 'manifesto' for TMB can be downloaded. TMB is endorsed by the DTI and supported by sponsors such as BT and Intel

- ☐ Supplying Government
  A part of the Office of Government Commerce that gives advice to businesses on selling products and services to government in England. A Get Connected! portal for government opportunities is planned

- ☐ Home Computing Initiatives (HCI)
  A scheme that allows companies to loan computer equipment to employees for home use, free of income tax and National Insurance liability

☐ Centres of Vocational Excellence (CoVE)
  A network of training centres in England that includes IT training for adult workers.

independent organisations

There are many organisations that provide solid advice and services about buying and using IT. The following provide some of the most useful material, much of which is free.

☐ National Computing Centre (NCC)
  Primarily aimed at IT professionals, the NCC also provides best practice guidelines on aligning IT with business strategy and an annual benchmark of IT spending

☐ BuyIT
  A not-for-profit best practice networking group that provides 'thought leadership', early adopter experience and guidelines. Its website includes guides such as 'The CEO's framework for e-business' and a full set of documents on how to specify, acquire and manage IT systems

☐ Business Application Software Developers Association (BASDA)
  Although representing vendors of software such as accounting systems, BASDA publishes documents such as a booklet on upgrading business systems and one on using the 'request for information' process for selecting a system. It is also active in standards work, in areas such as electronic procurement, VAT reporting and converting systems to handle the euro

☐ Independent Association of Accountants Information Technology Consultants (IAAITC)
  As its name suggests this organisation is a network for accountancy firms and aims to promote unbiased IT advice to clients

☐ CIO Connect
  A networking organisation for IT managers with a focus on the business opportunities presented by technology.

consultants/analysts

As one would expect, business and IT alignment have been a preoccupation of the big consultancies, and there are also smaller firms with some very useful material.

Here is a selection:

- ☐ Accenture – includes much material in its research and insights section

- ☐ IT-Director.com – an online resource published by Bloor Research

- ☐ IT Governance – a consultancy that specialises in IT project governance issues and publishes various reports and books including *IT Governance: Guidelines for Directors*

- ☐ Quocirca – a UK-based firm that focuses on both business and IT

It is also worth checking the websites of Forrester Research, Gartner, Ovum and other global IT analysts.

IT suppliers

The quality of advice provided by the major vendors, in particular, has improved greatly in recent years as they focus more on the SME market. In the UK, sites with a wealth of information include:

- ☐ Oracle
  The major software company and sponsor of this guide has grouped a good set of resources on the UK SME portion of its website. Included are white papers and articles on return on investment, funding and a 10 step process for SME success from research firm Datamonitor. There are also case studies, a free IT health check (see page 74) and access to a network of hundreds of software solutions. For more information, visit www.oracle.com/start and enter keyword 'success'.

- ☐ BT
  The telecoms firm has a lot of good technology advice on its website, although it can take some searching out. Content includes the well produced *Talking Business* magazine, also available in printed form

- Cisco Systems
  The networking provider has good online 'e-seminars' on topics such as financial management in the SME section of its UK website.

There are of course hundreds of suppliers active in the IT market – far too many even to categorise here. See page 77 for broad guidance on selecting an IT partner.

return on investment

Companies that offer tools and information on return on investment on IT include:

- Alinean
  A US firm with ROI tools and good resources on its website

- Cognizant
  US firm that provides ITEM (IT Effectiveness Measurement and Analysis Methodology)

- Shark Finesse
  A British company that provides a tool primarily aimed at vendor sales teams. It shows how value is calculated in an IT solution – the aim is for end users to plug in 'real world' values to arrive at a realistic projection. See worked example in resource section on page 75

other resources

- AbilityNet
  A charity that promotes computer technology for people with disabilities

- AccountingWeb
  An online accountants' resource with an IT zone

- eCommerce Innovation Centre
  Based at Cardiff University, the centre was one of the first to study e-commerce and to develop awareness among businesses

- e-consultancy
  A good resource for online marketing and e-commerce

☐ Flexibility
A magazine style website that covers issues such as technology for mobile and remote working

☐ GS1 UK
An authority on cross-sector supply chain standards

☐ Startups
A website with several categories of IT advice, including e-business and broadband

☐ Telecoms Advice
A source of practical information on communications technologies and doing business online

media

Look out for supplements on IT aimed at SMEs published in newspapers such as the *Guardian*, *Daily Telegraph*, *Sunday Times* and *Times*. Trade magazines are also a good source of material, especially those that serve the accountancy and sales and marketing professions.

IT media providers with online and/or printed publications include:

☐ *Computer Weekly* – IT news and management

☐ Silicon.com – a good selection of IT news and reports

☐ VNU – an IT news site that also emails a newsletter for SMEs

☐ ZDnet – IT news site that includes IT toolkits for smaller businesses

☐ The Register – a lively IT news site

the wheel turns

Professor Jim Norton, senior policy adviser on e-business and e-government for the IoD, highlights the predicted trends that will shape information and communication technologies in the coming years

Predicting the future is a dangerous game – if technology prophets were that good, they would all be rich and retired. However, there are some well-established trends that can be relied on, plus some new risks and options just starting to appear. Together these are likely to shape the envelope of opportunity for the profitable business exploitation of information and communications technologies (ICT) over the next 10 years.

well-established trends

hardware

The performance per unit cost of the electronic hardware used in processing, communicating and storing information will continue to grow exponentially. It has doubled 33 times over the last 55 years; in other words it doubles roughly every 20 months. This is the famous Moore's Law identified by Gordon Moore of Intel in 1965. It will double at least five times more with technology that is already understood today. Similarly, the performance per unit cost of fibre optic communications continues to double every eight months and has achieved 32 doublings since

> EXECUTIVE SUMMARY
> - software will mature into a professional engineering discipline
> - only companies that recognise the need to invest in, and attend to, organisational and people issues will succeed
> - the continued increase in access to affordable broadband will yield further opportunities for businesses, but also bring greater risks
> - an improved version of the application service provider model is likely to enjoy widespread uptake by SMEs

1982. Finally, the performance per unit cost of magnetic storage continues to double every 18 months, having achieved 26 doublings since 1965.

software

While software has not enjoyed the dramatic reductions witnessed in cost per unit performance of hardware, costs are being contained. The days of bespoke software are past, and now it's the ability to take largely standardised packages and configure these to meet individual company needs that is key. The next few years will see a welcome focus on improving the underlying quality and interoperability of these software packages, particularly in terms of security and reliability. What we will see is the development of software as it matures into a professional engineering discipline, rather than the 'black art' that it all too commonly represents today.

business change and information systems skills

Academic bookshelves groan under the weight of books written over the last 40 years that stress that there is no such thing as an information systems project that is isolated from the people who will use that system. There are only 'business change projects' comprising an integration of people and information technology with all the organisational politics, personal agendas, fears and mixed motivations that we human beings bring.

A stream of reports over the last five years have emphasised that too often the procurers of such change projects regard the people who will operate and use these systems as a necessary evil, rather than an integral part of the overall system design. Major failures are regularly paraded before the media. Such problems are invariably presented as either failure of the technology itself or of its suppliers, whereas in practice, it's more often a result of insufficient weight being given to organisational and people issues.

In terms of the predictable trends, the 'people' costs of business change will continue to grow sharply, while the relative costs of both hardware and software will fall. Why else would the major ICT hardware and software companies be moving so heavily into services?

A key success factor for the next ten years will be realistic and holistic budgeting, providing the necessary human and financial resources to implement new best practice. However, the traditional equipment-centred habit of not budgeting centrally for the large costs of people and process issues – both during procurement and in-service – will not be easily overturned.

In practice, these organisation and people change elements require at least as much funding (if not more) than contracting for the ICT equipment and software. They include:

- determination of end-user requirements, satisfaction surveys, business process re-engineering
- operating costs, personnel selection and security, job and team redesign
- organisation restructuring
- interoperability
- overcoming cultural resistance
- training
- rebuilding performance measurement and pay structures
- challenging disincentives in old business models, creating champions

Of concern is a growing skills crisis – particularly for smaller businesses – where access to information systems, project management and business change skills is increasingly difficult and expensive.

emerging developments

affordable broadband access

At the end of 2004, there were more than 150m affordable broadband access lines operating around the world with more than 50m installed during that year. There are now more than seven million such lines in the UK, with strong growth continuing.

This new form of access has had a dramatic impact on small and medium enterprises (SMEs), as for the first time it has provided 'always on' capability, in a cost-effective way. This has been a boon, with many SMEs buying broadband access for the simplest of reasons – to cut cost – but quickly recognising its potential to improve existing business processes by opening up entirely new opportunities. In an IoD/Nildram survey of members published in October 2004, 84 per cent of respondents with broadband indicated that they had achieved quantifiable productivity improvements. Thirty three per cent also cited measured improvement in customer satisfaction.

networked security

Sadly, silver linings often have black clouds hovering nearby and broadband is no exception. Vast numbers of PCs are now connected to high capacity 'always on' access and are not always secure. The same IoD/Nildram study revealed that 90 per cent of respondents with broadband access had installed protective firewalls, which means that 10 per cent remain totally vulnerable. Similarly, only 77 per cent of respondents kept on top of installing security updates. In general, IoD members' companies fared better than most SMEs, where security adoption rates are even lower. As a consequence, an enormous amount of broadband-attached distributed processing around the world is vulnerable to infection by 'malware' (viruses, worms, etc. installing Trojan horses, key logging and a variety of other malign software). Such infection will often occur within 20 minutes of an unprotected PC being attached to a broadband connection.

what might the future hold?

This combination of existing and emerging trends suggests that we might be about to see the rise of new information systems architectures that are based on more centralised processing. (This means less capability in potentially vulnerable end devices such as PCs.) This is the world of 'application service provision' (ASP) and so-called 'thin clients'. First mooted at the end of the nineties, this model was given a solid 'thumbs down', particularly by SMEs, since at that time the basis of trust in both communications and processing providers did not exist. Many directors could still remember picking up the telephone and not always getting a 'dial tone'. They were simply not interested in being sold the equivalent of a 'computer tone'. Similarly, cost-effective access to the necessary broadband connections was simply not available.

This is now changing. Research published by the IoD in the autumn of 2004 suggested that SMEs were now much more open to the idea of having basic services (such as an 'Office' desktop) or applications hosted remotely. If the necessary very high levels of availability and security can be unambiguously demonstrated, and trust established, this model offers real advantages for SMEs. It addresses the crucial issue of information systems skills shortage and offers a major advance on the vexed security and business continuity questions.

The ASP model will also allow access, on a per-user per-hour basis, to the complex supply chain management applications increasingly mandatory in dealing electronically with large companies.

The wheel turns. Those of us with long memories might recall the 'time sharing' computing models of the seventies and reflect that, perhaps we've seen some of this before.

IT healthcheck

The following questions can also be found at www.oracle.com/start (enter keyword 'success'). On completing the online questionnaire a benchmark report will be emailed to you showing how your company compares with others of your size and highlights how IT and e-business can support your business.

1. do you use computers in your business?

2. do you have Internet access for business purposes?

3. do you use email for business purposes?

4. do you use web access in the business?

5. do you use IT/the Internet to market products and services?

6. do you have an intranet (secure web site for exclusive use within your organisation)?

7. do you use IT/the Internet for purchasing indirect goods (goods used by your company but that are not actually made into a finished product)?

8. do you use IT/the Internet for purchasing direct goods (raw materials)?

9. do you use IT/the Internet to exchange documents with suppliers?

10. do you have broadband access for business?

11. do you use IT/the Internet for supporting customers?

12. do you use IT/the Internet to exchange documents with customers?

13. did you recruit/try to recruit IT specialists in the past 12 months?

14. do you use IT/the Internet for human resources (HR) management?

15. do you have an extranet (secure website that can be extended out to partners, suppliers and customers as required)?

16. do you have wireless access to the company's computer systems?

17. do you use IT/the Internet to automate expenses reporting?

18. do you use IT/the Internet for employee training (e-learning)?

19. do you use IT/the Internet for selling?

20. do you use IT/the Internet to collaborate and forecast product demand?

return on investment – a worked example

The following is a worked example of how a company made a realistic projection on its return on investment using a software tool provided by Shark Finesse (www.sharkfinesse.com).

A UK stationery distribution business had operational problems caused by inefficient 'legacy' systems. New resource planning software would run its business more effectively but the directors needed evidence that the cost of the system would be more than covered by future economic benefits. The solution would take six months to implement so no benefits would accrue until seven months after the initial purchase. Also, the business required at least 10 per cent returns per annum on this extra spend.

OVERVIEW

Solution cost	£300,000
Monthly maintenance and support, etc.	£4,000
Minimum annual return requirement	10 per cent
Period of review	48 months
Total investment of £492,000 over the four-year period.	

By reaching agreement on realistic – not over-optimistic – figures, this spend was justified by the following economic benefits(in the box below):

ECONOMIC BENEFITS

☐ stationery savings	£26,000 per annum – the legacy solution could only be printed onto non-standard documents
☐ outgoing IT supplier	£36,000 per annum in support charges saved
☐ stock obsolescence	£100,000 per annum – better visibility of slow stock, avoiding reorder of slow items, special incentives/procurement
☐ faster cash collection	A two-day improvement in cash collection for this £80m turnover business. The interest savings were £44,000 a year

These benefits, only valued from month seven onwards, delivered the following returns :

- [ ] payback 30 months
- [ ] IRR (rate of return) 28 per cent per annum
- [ ] NPV (increase in shareholder value) £123,157

The solution – which everybody in the business wanted from a technical point of view – was therefore supported by a business justification to make the decision quickly, and fend off the risk of 'doing nothing'.

selecting a supplier

The following are key attributes that any supplier should have:

☐ technology skills

Often SMEs hire an IT services provider to supply specific skills they lack in-house. Ensure that any potential provider possesses the required skill in abundance. Meet the project team in advance and check that they have certification for the technology area you're looking for. Look for evidence of strong partnerships with IT vendors, such as elevated membership of vendor partner programmes.

☐ knowing your business

The provider should have a good knowledge and experience of companies like yours, in your industry. It is crucial they understand your business and the operational pressures you face. Ask for examples of where they have worked with other companies of your size in your sector.

☐ ability to deliver

SMEs commonly look for an IT partner that can take full responsibility for a project. Be mindful of physical location – the nearer the provider is based the more time it will be able to devote to you and form a lasting relationship, and it will be better able to cope with unexpected or late night call-outs.

☐ strategic thinking

Many smaller companies think of IT in terms of a necessary cost, rather than as a strategic, profit-generating asset. A good IT services provider will act not just as an implementer but also as an adviser on the most strategic and advantageous use of technology.

☐ flexibility

Technology vendors are particularly keen to do more business in the SME market. Businesses should exploit this by looking for innovative financing deals and extra 'bundled' functionality and service.

☐ return on investment

Sometimes companies forget that one reason they hired the provider was to save on the cost of recruiting and maintaining in-house staff. It helps to know in advance what, financially, you want to achieve with any new system.

useful websites

AbilityNet
www.abilitynet.co.uk

Accenture
www.accenture.com

AccountingWeb
www.accountingweb.co.uk

Alinean
www.alinean.com

BT
www.bt.com

Business Application Software Developers Association (BASDA)
www.basda.org

Business Link
www.businesslink.gov.uk

Centres of Vocational Excellence
www.cove.lsc.gov.uk

CIO Connect
www.cio-connect.com

Cisco Systems
www.cisco.com/uk

Computer Weekly
www.computerweekly.com

DTI Best Practice
www.dti.gov.uk/bestpractice

eCommerce Innovation centre
www.ecommerce.ac.uk

e-consultancy
www.e-consultancy.com

Flexibility
www.flexibility.co.uk

GS1 UK
www.gs1uk.org

Home Computing Initiatives
www.ukhomecomputing.co.uk

Independent Association of Accountants Information Technology
Consultants (IAAITC).
www.iaaitc.org

IT Director (Bloor Research)
www.IT-director.com

IT Governance
www.itgovernance.co.uk

National Computing Centre (NCC)
www.ncc.co.uk

Oracle
www.oracle.com/start and enter keyword 'success'

Quocirca
www.quocirca.com

The Register
www.theregister.co.uk

Shark Finesse
www.sharkfinesse.com

Silicon.com
www.silicon.com

Startups
www.startups.co.uk

Supplying Government
www.supplyinggovernment.gov.uk

Technology Means Business
www.tmb.org.uk

Telecoms Advice
www.telecoms.advice.org.uk

VNU
www.vnunet.com

ZDnet
www.zdnet.co.uk

WHO SAID:
YOU HAD TO CHOOSE A NEW IT SUPPLIER EACH TIME A NEW IT SOLUTION IS REQUIRED?

Name: _____

Title: _____

Address: _____

Job: _____

Company name: _____

Postcode: _____

Email: _____

Telephone: _____

Business solutions – please send me information on...

Core e-Business software applications

- [ ] Financial Management
- [ ] Order Management
- [ ] Field Sales
- [ ] Purchasing Management
- [ ] Discrete Manufacturing
- [ ] TeleService
- [ ] Inventory Management
- [ ] TeleSales
- [ ] Daily Business Intelligence

- [ ] Supplier / customer portals – Oracle Fusion Middleware / Oracle Database 10g
- [ ] Funding – Oracle Finance
- [ ] Hosted solutions – Oracle On Demand
- [ ] Collaboration and file sharing – Oracle Collaboration Suite
- [ ] Industry and specialist software – Oracle Partners Solutions Catalogue

For FREE resources and case studies – visit
www.oracle.com/start and type in key word: **success**

■ FREE Oracle Internet Seminar – Becoming an e-Business (16 mins)

■ FREE Trial CD of Oracle Database 10g Standard Edition One

■ 10 Step Strategy for SME success – Report by Datamonitor

WIN

Complete & return this reply card by the 30th September 2005 for your chance to win one of four 4GB Apple iPod Minis in Silver.

Participation in the sweepstakes is subject to official rules which may be viewed at www.oracle.com/start and enter keyword: success

Oracle Corporation UK Ltd
Wyvern House
Wyvern Way
Rockingham Road
Uxbridge
UB8 2XN